BLUFF YOUR WAY IN PHILOSOPHY

Jim Hankinson

CENTENNIAL PRESS

ISBN 0-8220-2221-4
U.S. edition Copyright © 1990 by Centennial Press
British edition Copyright © 1985 by The Bluffer's Guides

Printed in U.S.A.
All Rights Reserved

Centennial Press, Box 82087, Lincoln, Nebraska 68501
an imprint of Cliffs Notes, Inc.

INTRODUCTION

What Philosophy Is

The cardinal rule for amateur bluffer-philosophers is: never *ever* try to explain what philosophy "is." Philosophy isn't a subject—it's an activity. One doesn't "study" it per se; one *does* it. This is how philosophers, at least those in the Anglo-Saxon tradition (which for some obscure historical reason seems to include the Finns), tend to explain it. In other words, philosophy is largely a matter of *conceptual analysis*—or thinking about thinking.

Concerning what philosophy is, stick to basics. This is something most philosophers find temperamentally impossible, but there's no reason you should follow suit. Most people are awed by philosophers, and philosophy itself seems bewilderingly complex to them. This is all to your advantage. Keep 'em confused. Even philosophers themselves, with a few exceptions, find it almost impossible to speak a language (such as English) that's comprehensible to the ordinary lay person. A philosopher wanting even to refer to the Ordinary Lay Person (a species with which he is unlikely to have had first-hand acquaintance, although he may have heard travelers' tales about them) will think of him as just one more Ward Cleaver type—totally unaware that the Ward and June stereotypes are now black and rich and have the No. 1-ranked sitcom.

3

Your assignment, therefore (if you choose to accept it), is to get at least a semi-tenuous grip on some of the technical vocabulary that's used by the contemporary philosophers. Don't worry. Linguistic competence, as the later Wittgenstein would have said (not to be confused, of course, with the earlier Wittgenstein, who wouldn't have agreed) is a matter of getting words in the right order. As long as you get the words in the right order, you won't actually have to understand what (if anything) it all means.

LIVES OF THE PHILOSOPHERS

Philosophy is a subject (*sorry*, an activity) with a history, and because philosophy makes so little progress (if indeed if makes any at all), its history is consequently more important than that of other fields. The successful bluffer must be armed with at least a skeletal knowledge of this history if he or she is to make a real success of charlatanry. Thus, we'll confine ourselves almost exclusively to Western philosophy, that tradition begun in Greece in the seventh century B.C. There's a good reason for this. Philosophy in the Western tradition is very different from that of the Orient. However, in a later section, we'll give some advice on how to be marginally knowledgeable about such matters as Meditation, Buddhism, Indian Religions, People with Shaved Heads in Grubby Yellow Robes, and similar tangents of faith.

This section contains some more or less interesting facts about some more or less famous philosophers, of both a biographical and a philosophical nature, in a roughly chronological order.

The first Greek philosophers are known generally, if misleadingly, as the **pre-Socratics.** Misleadingly, as not all of them came before **Socrates,** and in any case they formed no coherent school. Many of them, in fact, didn't even form coherent individuals. No one knows why philosophy even started when it did. Ambitious bluffers with Marxist tendencies could try to account for it in terms of an inexorable dialetic of historical forces, but we wouldn't recommend it. A notable feature of many of the pre-Socratics is their attempt to reduce the material constituents of the Universe to one or more basic Stuffs—such as Earth, Air, Fire, Water, Sardines, Ex-Lax, etc.

Thales of Miletus (ca. 620–550 B.C.) was the first recognized philosopher. There may have been others before him, but no one knows who they were. He's remembered chiefly for two philosophical claims:

(1) Everything is made of water.
(2) Magnets have souls.

Not an auspicious start, but it was a beginning.

Anaximander (ca. 610–550 B.C.) thought everything was made of the Unlimited, a concept which has a certain cosmic appeal, until you realize that it's absolutely meaningless. You'll score more bluffing points if you remember that he was one of the first to try to draw a map of the world.

Anaximenes (ca. 570–510 B.C.) struck out boldly in a new direction; he said everything was really made of air, a view perhaps more plausible in Greece than, for instance, in the yellow smog of Los Angeles.

Heraclitus (ca. 540–490 B.C.) agreed with Anaximenes about air, but he went a stage further, claiming that everything was in a state of flux—that you couldn't step into the same river twice, and that there was no difference between Up and Down, both of which are proof that he'd never been white-water rafting on the Snake River. In passing (always the best way to refer to things in philosophy), it's sometimes worthwhile to refer to "Heraclitus's Metaphysic," just another name for his theory about flux, as long as there's no danger of your having to explain yourself.

Pythagoras (ca. 570–510 B.C.), as every schoolchild knows, invented the right triangle; in fact, he went further, believing that everything was made of numbers. He also believed in an extreme form of reincarnation, holding that a wide variety of improbable things, including shrubs and beans, had souls, which made his diet problematic and was probably indirectly responsible for his bizarre death.

Empedocles (ca. 492–432 B.C.), a notable fifth-century Sicilian political wheeler-dealer, physician, and oddball (see next section on Deaths for details), thought everything was made of Earth, Air, Fire, and Water, held together (or broken down) by Love and Strife, each taking turns to get the upper hand in a cycle of eternal recurrence, sort of a cosmic *As the World Turns.*

Then we get the **Eleatics: Parmenides** (ca. 520–430 B.C.) and **Melissus** (ca. 480–420 B.C.). Instead of contending that everything was in fact made of one substance or several substances, they held that there was, in reality, only one Thing—large, spherical, infinite, motionless, and changeless. All appearance of variety, motion, separateness of objects, etc., is an Illusion.

Their successor, **Zeno of Elea** (ca. 500–440 B.C.), advanced a series of paradoxical arguments to the effect that nothing can move. His story about Achilles and the Tortoise is still discussed, as is his story about the arrow, in which he argued that it (the arrow), couldn't possibly move. Sebastian would *not* have agreed. Zeno's arguments rest mainly on the question of whether Space and Time are infinitely divisible, or whether one or both are made up of indivisible *quanta.*

Mention these ideas to give Zeno a contemporary relevance. If called upon to back it up, change the subject.

Last among the pre-Socratics come the **Atomists: Democritus** (ca. 450–360 B.C.) and **Leucippus** (ca. 450–390 B.C.). They're sometimes held responsible for anticipating modern atomic theories. This is garbage, and you can always score some points by saying so. The Atomists said that atoms can't be split, whereas today we know all too well that they can be. You might also point out that Democritus didn't like sex, unlike his highly sexed teacher Leucippus, who repeatedly said, "I do what I do because I *need* to."

So much for the pre-Socratics. Now for The Man himself, **Socrates** (ca. 469–399 B.C.). Socrates didn't write anything, so we have to rely on Plato for information about him, and it's uncertain how accurately Plato reproduced Socrates' own views and how much of his own material he attributed to Socrates. Don't get embroiled in arguing the matter; it's far better to say, with a certain understated contempt, that philosophical *content* is what matters, *not* its historical provenance.

Plato (ca. 427–347 B.C.) believed that ordinary, everyday objects like tables and chairs are merely imperfect, flawed "phenomenal" copies of perfect Originals that are laid up in Heaven to be appreciated by the intellect, the so-called Forms. There are also Forms of abstract items, such as Truth, Beauty, Goodness, Love, Overdrafts, etc. This particular theory got Plato into trouble; if everything we see, feel, touch, etc., has its real existence in some Perfect Form, there must be Perfectly Good Forms of Perfectly Awful Things. Plato himself mentions hair, mud, and filth; we can think of better

8

examples, such as oil portraits of Elvis on black velvet and dusty, plastic, dashboard saints.

Plato is grossly overrated as a philosopher. The following is a typical Platonic argument, from Book 2 of the *Republic*.

(1) Anyone who distinguishes between things on the grounds of knowledge (as opposed, presumably, to mere prejudice) is a philosopher.
(2) Guard dogs distinguish between things according to whether or not they know them (this is a truth well known to Avon ladies and postal carriers); ergo
(3) All guard dogs are philosophers.

Try that one on for size sometime.

Another useful ploy with Plato is to argue that

(1) he was a feminist, or
(2) he wasn't.

Both claims can be supported, and each may turn out to be handy (at different times, of course). The evidence for No. 1 is that, in Book 3 of the *Republic,* he says that women should *not* be discriminated against in matters of employment solely because they are women. To buttress your argument for No. 2, state that Plato remarks that since women are so much *less* talented than men by their very nature, this "liberalization" (conceded in No. 1) will make hardly any difference anyway.

After Plato comes **Aristotle** (ca. 384–322 B.C.), sometimes known as the Stagyrite, which is not something you find dangling from an underground cavern, or an obscure sexual deviation, but a native of Stagira in Macedonia. He was a pupil of Plato's, and he expected to succeed him as head of the Academy. Accordingly, he got his nose out of joint when **Speusippus** (no need to know anything about him) got the job. So he went off in a huff to establish his own school, the Lyceum. Aristotle was disgustingly brilliant—like all those smart-asses that screw up the grading curve. He made contributions to Logic (in fact, he invented it), Philosophy of Science (he invented that too), Biological Taxonomy (yes, he invented that as well), Ethics, Political Philosophy, Semantics, Aesthetics, Theory of Rhetoric, Cosmology, Meteorology, Dynamics, Hydrostatics, Theory of Mathematics, and Home Economics. (His wife claimed, however, that he was incapable of tying his own necktie, and she had to do it for him—just kidding, neckties weren't even invented then.)

Don't be tempted to say something outright uncomplimentary about Aristotle, but the confident bluffer *might* comment, *sotto voce*, about the excessively teleological bias of his Biology or remark that, despite all of his logical theories, they've all been superceded by modern developments—accomplished, for the most part, by men like Frege and Russell (*q.v.*). But take care. Never use this line in conversation with a mathematician, even a young one.

A fairly safe course to follow is to be moderately disparaging about the more ludicrous aspects of Aristotle's Biology, such as his conclusion concerning the structure of a snake's genitalia:

> Snakes have no penis because they have no legs; and they have no testicles because they are so long.
> *De Generatione Animalium*

He offers no argument to support the first contention, except one supposes the snake would have to drag it

10

painfully along the ground, but the second notion derives from his reproductive theory. For Aristotle, semen is not produced in the testicles, but in the spinal column (the testicles function apparently as a sort of roadside rest area for the traveling sperm); furthermore, cold semen is infertile, and the further it has to travel, the colder it gets (hence the well-known fact, he remarks, that men with long penises are infertile). So, given that snakes are so long, if the semen stopped off to rest anywhere on the way, snakes would be infertile. But they aren't; therefore, they have no testicles. A real humdinger of an argument. And an example of excessive teleology, which in this instance really means getting the whole thing back to where we were when we began.

After Aristotle, philosophy gets increasingly fragmented. Several rival schools were formed to complement and compete with the already existing Academy and Lyceum. The major new arrivals at the beginning of the third century B.C. are the **Stoics,** the **Epicureans** and the **Skeptics.**

The **Stoics** believed, perversely, in an all-embracing Divine Providence, in spite of all evidence to the contrary—such as the occurrence of natural disasters, the prevalence of injustice, and the existence of hemorrhoids. **Chrysippus,** perhaps the most prominent and certainly the most verbose of the Stoics, argued that bedbugs had been created by a Benevolent Provider to stop people from oversleeping. The Stoics also made important developments in logical theory, which enabled them to formulate types of arguments that had eluded Aristotle. But you shouldn't worry too much about that.

The **Epicureans**, named after their founder **Epicurus** (ca. 342–270 B.C.), held that pleasure was the End, what we all strive for, and that this consisted in the satisfaction of desires—which was a good start. But then they had to foul things up by arguing that this didn't mean that a *lot* of pleasure was a good thing. You should limit the number of desires that you had so you wouldn't get left with a lot of *un*satisfied ones. This obviously results in a miserably dull life (and would certainly put a cramp in the bedtime fantasies of the average adolescent).

Epicureanism is a logical point of view, radically opposed to that view of philosophy which sees the End as essentially a pursuit of the Ineffable and Unattainable—the Mystic Union with the Creator, Total Empathy with the Cosmos, an Affair with Valerie Bertinelli.

Concerning "pleasure," Epicureans said,

> By pleasure we mean the absence of mental and physical pain. It isn't a matter of boozing, orgiastic parties, or indulgence in women, small boys, or fish.
>
> (from the *Letter to Menoeceus*)

We don't know where he came up with fish (as opposed to sheep), but we assure you that it's in the text. The other important feature of Epicureanism was their version of Atomic Theory, which was a lot like Democritus's, except that, in order to preserve Free Will, they held that every now and again atoms swerved unpredictably, causing collisions, somewhat like bumper cars. They also held that although the gods existed, they didn't give a damn about human affairs because they had better things to do. (Probably because

they were more interested in the affairs that they themselves were having.)

The other major school of the period, the **Skeptics,** didn't believe anything. Their founder, **Pyrrho of Elis** (ca. 360–270 B.C.), didn't write any books (presumably because he didn't believe anyone would read them if he did), although later Skeptics (backsliding Skeptics) did so, notably **Timon,** who wrote a book of clever satires called the *Silli, Aenesidemus,* and *Sextus Empiricus.* In general, these men argued that *none* of our senses was trustworthy, though they *might* register pleasure, so, consequently, you couldn't be sure of anything. Indeed, you couldn't be sure of the fact that you couldn't be sure of anything.

It's said that Pyrrho's skepticism was so strong that friends repeatedly had to stop him from walking off cliffs, under passing chariots, and into rivers, which must have been a full-time job, although they seem to have been pretty good at it, as he lived to a ripe old age. He's said to have visited the Indian Gymnosophists, or "naked philosophers," so-called because of their habit of conducting nude seminars. It's recorded that he once got so irritated by repeated public questioning that he stripped off his clothes (which was perhaps the only influence that the Gymnosophists had on him), leaped into the illusory River Alphaeus, and swam away.

At that time, there were some minor schools struggling to be recognized as bastions of philosophical wisdom, and among them were the **Cynics,** masters of the snide remark and SOB's at dinner parties. One of them, **Crates,** was known as "the Gate-crasher" because of his habit of bursting into people's houses and insulting them (referred to later as the Don Rickles school of comedy). The most famous Cynic was **Diogenes,** who lived in a barrel to avoid paying rent, and once memorably, if rashly, told Alexander the Great to get out of his light. He also scandalized people by eating, having sex, and masturbating in public places whenever the mood struck him.

Pretend to like the Cynics. They didn't give diddly squat what anyone else thought of them and are consequently a model of the Philosophic Temperament or a smart-ass — depending on your point of view. It doesn't really matter what your point of view is, but be sure to have one.

Time passed and philosophy dottered on in the Greco-Roman world, under the unpredictable patronage of the Roman emperors, whose attitudes towards philosophers varied considerably. Marcus Aurelius, for instance, was a philosopher himself; Nero, on the other hand, killed philosophers (which was the singularly dominating reason why philosophy was considered a poor-risk profession to get into at that time). The influence of Christianity began to be felt in this period, and philosophy began to suffer.

Augustine, for some bizarre reason, became a saint — in spite of his prodigal sex life and his famous prayer to God: "Make me chaste — but not just yet." Interestingly, he anticipated Descartes' famous Cogito remark "I think, therefore I am." *Always* refer to it as "The Cogito" (as in "The Donald"). He also developed a theory of time in which God stood *outside* the temporal stream of events (being Eternal and Unchangeable, he had little choice, really), and because he was Unchangeable and Eternal, he never knew what time anything was. Rather like today's average philosophy professor.

In those days, tending to their flocks of disciples, there were also the **Neoplatonists,** some of whom were Christians and some of whom weren't, and these latter all had names which began with "P." The Christians among them were obsessed with the notion that Plato had really been a Christian, an idea requiring a startling, not to say implausible, temporal reorganization. Neoplatonists tended to talk of Abstract Things with Capital Letters, such as the One and Being, in a way that no one could understand. This fault, by the way, isn't confined to them. **Heidegger** did it as well, but then he was a German, and you have to expect that sort of thing from the Germans. You'll come across some people who profess an admiration for this group, so don't hesitate to dismiss them out of hand, especially **Plotinus, Porphyry,** and **Proclus,** though you may allow, grudgingly, that the latter had some interesting ideas about Causes.

After that came the Dark Ages, and the "flame of philosophy," as verbose historians are inclined to label it, was kept alive in the Arab world (of all places) and in monasteries that were either too remote or too poverty-stricken to be worth sacking. Not surprisingly, philosophy, insofar as it existed in Europe at all, took a depressingly theological turn, focusing on the question of whether God was One Person in Three or Three People in One, the exact nature of the Substance of the Holy Spirit, and how many angels could dance on the tongue of a termite (62, provided they aren't doing the boogaloo).

It's worth mentioning Cordoba in southern Spain,

which, under the Arab occupation, was the home of the great Jewish philosopher **Maimonides** and the great Arab philosopher **Averroës.** Some argue (a bluffer's point or two to know something about) that **Avicenna,** not Averroës, was the greatest Arab philosopher, but don't give an inch. (Dogmatism pays.) For several hundred years, Jews, Arabs, and Christians lived together there. Religious intolerance, though perennial, has not been an invariable fact of life.

Philosophy in Europe began to revive in the eleventh century with **Anselm,** another of the philosophical saints. Anselm is famous for having invented the misleadingly named Ontological Argument for the existence of God. This "argument" is remarkable because it's absolutely implausible, its longevity is legendary, and you can't really refute it. It goes like this: think of a being that embodies perfection (no, not Jessica Hahn), a being that no other can excel in greatness. But existence itself is a property that enhances greatness.* So if this greatest thing (i.e., God) doesn't exist, there would be a yet greater thing imaginable, namely an existent God, having all the same properties as the other one—with the added bonus of existence. We can conceive this. So God must exist.

Anselm himself tells us that God sent this argument to him in a vision shortly after breakfast on July 13, 1087 (a Thursday), when his faith was wavering. It's thus the only major argument in philosophical history whose discovery can be precisely dated. Unless, of course, Anselm was pulling our leg.

---

*This contention, implausible when applied to halitosis and small children, becomes more persuasive if the entity in question is good in all other aspects.

The next important philosophical saint was **Thomas Aquinas** (1225–74), who was largely responsible for the reintroduction of Aristotle into the Western tradition. (He had been politely ignored for several centuries by scholars who didn't like to admit they couldn't understand Greek.) Thomas is also the only philosopher officially recognized by the Catholic Church. He's notable for propounding the Five Ways of proving the existence of God – he hadn't been much impressed with Anselm. You don't need to know what they are, but point out that there isn't much difference between the first three Ways, so Aquinas was overplaying his hand.

Thomas is also the author of two interesting arguments against incest. First, it would make family life even more hellishly complex than it is already, and second, incest between siblings should be forbidden because if the "love proper to husband and wife" were joined to that "appropriate between brother and sister," the resulting bond would be so powerful as to result in unnaturally rampant sexual intercourse. It's unfortunate that Thomas doesn't define this last intriguing concept. One might doubt that he ever had any brothers or sisters.

As for the rest of the medieval Schoolmen (as they are known from the pedagogic predilection for intense pedantry), most of the important ones seem to have been Franciscans. You should steer clear of them, at least in any detail. In passing (that phrase again), you might recall that **Duns Scotus** (1270–1308) was Scottish and was, in addition, according to Gerard Manley Hopkins, "of reality the rarest-veined unraveller," whatever that means. But it *is* impressive to roll that phrase off the tip of your tongue. Another name worth dropping is that of **William of Ockham** (ca. 1290–1349), by common consent the greatest of the medieval logicians and known for the invention of "Ockham's Razor," with which he put an end to centuries of rather hairy philosophy. A choice *bon mot* of William's was

Entities should not be multiplied beyond necessity.

In other words, don't muck up things if you don't have to. Or, cut the crap.

The modern age of philosophy effectively starts in the Renaissance with the discovery of **Greek Skepticism;** these philosophical diatribes were translated by **Lorenzo Valla** and put to good use by **Michel de Montaigne.** After ascending from Valla to Montaigne, **Skeptical Epistemology** formed the basis from which Descartes was able to rebuild a positive philosophy.

René Descartes (1596–1650), as almost every first-year philosophy student will tell you, was the Father of Modern Philosophy. In many ways (despite the fact that he was a philosopher), he was a highly engaging character: he had enormous difficulty getting up in the morning (one of those guys), and he invented the Cogito (remember, *always* call it that) while hiding in a store in Bavaria in 1620 to avoid military service. He never married but had an illegitimate daughter.

It's advisiable to memorize Descartes' famous philosophical slogan, the Cogito, in at least three languages; you won't get much mileage out of it in English. Descartes himself published in both Latin and French: "Cogito ergo sum"; "Je pense, donc je suis" (the French version is from *Discours de la Méthode,* which is less well known than the Latin *Meditations* and consequently better material for the bluffer). Advanced bluffers can amuse themselves by supplying versions in German, Serbo-Croatian, Urdu, etc. Descartes came to the conclusion that this at least was certain, after systematically trying to doubt everything else, starting with comparatively simple things — like navel oranges, cream cheese, real numbers, and gradually working up to the really tough concepts, like his landlady and God.

Descartes discovered that he could doubt the existence of everything except the reality of his own thoughts. (He was even a bit doubtful about his own body, and with good reason, if contemporary portraits are anything to go by.) From his unshakeable certainty, he proceeded to "rebuild a metaphysical bridge" (use the phrase; it sounds weighty and philosophical) back into ordinary reality, by way of a proof of the existence of God (quite how needn't concern you; it's enough to know that he did). In the end, he left things pretty much the way he'd found them. But philosophy's like that, as Wittgenstein was to point out. You may legitimately wonder whether it's worth the bother. But don't wonder aloud.

From this point on, philosophy begins to show signs of splitting into two traditions, the British and the Continental. This sort of remark enrages the French and Germans, who, not unreasonably, like to think of their individual traditions as being separate — so it comes in handy when talking to them.

The British tend to be lumped together as the **Empiricists,** which, as the name suggests, means that they created their systems from the basis of what could be *felt, observed,* and *experienced.* The important figures sound like an ethnic joke: there was an Englishman (**Locke**), an Irishman (**Berkeley**), and a Scotsman

(**Hume**). Despite the stereotypes, however, Berkeley was very clever and Hume very generous.

But let's start with **John Locke** (1632–1704), who thought that objects had two kinds of attributes:

(1) Primary Qualities, such as Extension, Solidity, and Number, which are held to be inseparable from and inherent in the objects themselves, and

(2) Secondary Qualities, such as Color, Taste, and Smell, which *seem* to be in the objects, but are *in fact* in the percipient. (Anyone who has recently passed a field of freshly spread horse manure will see the fallacy of this notion.)

What you're supposed to do with such attributes as bathroom profanity, which seems to be both widespread and objective, no one's sure, but possibly Locke would say that Ugliness, like Beauty, is in the eye of the beholder, which means that there's hope for all of us.

Locke also thought that we have no Innate Ideas (thus, the infant mind is a *tabula rasa,* a clean slate — as indeed man's adult mind too often appears to be) and that all our knowledge of the external world is derived either directly from experience or indirectly by extrapolating from it. This gave him some trouble in accounting for highly abstract concepts like Number, Infinity, and Edible Fast Food. He also held interesting views on the problem of Personal Identity: How do I differentiate Myself from Other Minds? What is the content of the continuity of my Personality? Am I the same Person who married my wife five years ago? If so, is there anything *I* can do about it? All of these are fascinating speculations, contending that not all Men are Persons, for to be a Person requires a certain level of intelligent self-consciousness; thus, not all Persons are Men. His reason for believing this conclusion rested squarely on his credulous acceptance of a Latin American traveler's story about meeting an intelligent, Portuguese-speaking macaw in Rio de Janeiro.

George Berkeley (1685–1753), in spite of the disadvantages of being both Irish and a bishop, was more radical. He held that things exist only if perceived ("Esse est percipi"; try to remember that), and his reason for believing this extraordinary notion, which he seemed to think was simply common sense, was that it is impossible to think of something's being *un*perceived, for in the very act of trying to think of it as being unperceived, you are, by thinking of it, perceiving it.

Berkeley's philosophy was all the rage for a while and had the virtue of greatly irritating Dr. Johnson, who claimed to have refuted it by kicking a stone—a peculiarly unphilosophical form of refutation which completely missed Berkeley's point. People who subscribe to such views are called **Idealists** (*q.v.* Glossary). Like most things in philosophy, they have a certain lunatic following. G. E. Moore once remarked that Idealists believe trains have wheels only when they are in stations because they can't see them when they're on board. It also follows, interestingly, that people don't have bodies except when they're naked—a fact which, if true, would make a lot of everyday fantasizing a waste of time.

The natural successor to views of this sort is a kind of Skepticism, and this is where **Hume** (1711–76) comes in. Hume published his first book, the *Treatise of Human Nature,* in 1739 and was a tad irritated when no one took any notice of it. Undeterred, however, he simply rewrote it and issued it under another title, *Inquiry into Human Understanding*, and it hit the best-seller lists. Most philosophers think that the *Inquiry* is far inferior to the *Treatise*; you might try opposing this view (the *Inquiry* has the virtue of being much shorter, for one thing).

Among the things that are useful to know about Hume is that he developed an original account of Causes, according to which, Cause and Effect are simply the names we give to events or items that have repeatedly been observed to go along with one another. In other words, "Constant Conjunction." Try pointing out that Hume's three formulations of this principle in the *Inquiry* are *not* equivalent. One makes causes *necessary* conditions for their effects; the second makes them *sufficient* conditions; the third seems to be ambiguous. And you might note that this principle can't differentiate between causes and collateral effects. (We do hope you're taking notes; you'll be tested on this at the end of the book.) Hume also thought Free Will and Determinism could be made compatible. Politely doubt this.

Meanwhile, back on the Continent, let's not neglect such an individual as **Spinoza** (1632–77), a Jewish lens grinder from Amsterdam. He was much admired (though not, apparently, by his contemporaries, who first publicly cursed him, then when that didn't work, tried to have him assassinated) for his Ethical System, which he set out like a set of formal deductions in geometry. Unsurprisingly, given his method, he was a strong **Determinist** and believed in unshakeable Logical Necessity.

The best way to bluff about Spinoza is to balance

admiration for the man with a sigh of disappointment that he used a philosophical system so unsuitable to the subject matter of ethics. Ethics, you point out, is not capable of exhibition in a formal, axiomatized system. That'll shut 'em up.

Leibniz (1646–1716) is popularly known as the man whom Voltaire caricatured as Pangloss in *Candide,* the optimistic twerp who thinks that everything's for the best in this best of all possible worlds — which is baloney, of course. However, Leibniz only wrote things like that to comfort monarchs. Otherwise, he wrote extensively on Logical and Metaphysical matters, but these speculations weren't published in his lifetime because they weren't very comforting to monarchs. In the unlikely event of his name coming up in a conversation, reflect sadly on the difference between the quality of Leibniz's private thoughts and the hollowness of his public pronouncements.

Space prevents us from saying much about the French philosophers of the eighteenth century, but you should know that the top men were **Voltaire, Rousseau,** and **Diderot.** All were remarkable for having been arrested or exiled — or both. It's becoming fashionable to extol Diderot's originality, good sense, humanity, and fine erotic prose at the expense of the others. He's worth cultivating for the good reason that virtually no one's read him in the original. Try dropping *Le Rêve de d'Alembert* or *Jacques Le Fataliste* into the conversation — and don't forget to mention that he wrote porn for a living.

The **Marquis de Sade** is always choice bluffing material, partly as an example of an extravagantly deviant, aristocratic scumbag and partly because of his brand of state-of-nature philosophy. His motto was "If it feels good, do it." It did, he did, and he was locked up for it. You could mention *Philosophie dans le Boudoir,* an extraordinary mixture of socio-biological political and moral philosophy and imaginatively choreographed sado-masochistic sex. You could wonder tentatively whether his philosophy has been taken seriously enough (it has; but you needn't mention that).

Which brings us up to the nineteenth-century Germans. Steer clear of them. All you need to know about their forerunner, **Kant,** can be found in another section (*q.v.* Ethics). All anyone really knows about **Hegel** could be written on the back of a postcard and even then would be unintelligible. Hegel had, in an advanced form, that talent common to lawyers, computer freaks, and German philosophers: making something that's basically simple ridiculously complex. He first used the word "dialectic" to mean the interplay of opposing historical forces and is thus important in the pre-history of Marxism. Apart from that, German philosophical terminology can be most impressive when properly used (see Glossary). Much the same goes for **Schopenhauer.**

Nietzsche (1844–1900) was a fascinating eccentric and is thus ideal for cocktail party chatter. Contemporary opinion brackets him with Wagner as a proto-fascist, and he was also anti-Semitic, but then so was virtually everyone else in ninteenth-century Prussia. He was repulsed by women and convinced that God was dead or at the very least was taking unauthorized time off. He also advanced a doctrine of Eternal Recurrence, according to which everything happens over and over again in exactly the same way—like congressional elections. He professed to find this comforting – proof that his elevator didn't stop on all floors. Imagine an eternity of repetitious tedium, each recurrence so *precisely* similar to all others that none contains memories of any of the others. Such notions don't bear repeating. (Think of it this way, imagine an eternity of watching *Gilligan's Island* interspersed with *The Love Boat.* The mind boggles at the thought.) Nietzsche finally went certifiably nuts in 1888 (some would say he had done so a great deal earlier) and began to write books with headings like *Why I'm So Clever* and *Why I Write Such Profound Books.*

Among the non-Germans of the nineteenth century, you should mention **Kierkegaard,** if only to prove that you know how to pronounce it: "Keer-ke-gore."

The most notable French philosopher of the period was **Henri Bergson.** He was a **Vitalist** – that is, he believed that what distinguished animate from inanimate matter was the presence in the former of some mysterious *Èlan Vital,* or Life Force, a strange and undefined Power which, for some reason, leaves the human body during adolescence. He also wrote a long book about laughter that didn't contain one good joke.

Which brings us to our own home-grown philosophers. The distinctive American contribution to philosophy at this time was Pragmatism, which says that Truth is not absolute; it's a matter of convention, or in a phrase much used by some modern philosophers, "Truth is up for grabs." This also points out its relevance to modern-day politics. This reliance on pragmatism was held by **William James** and **John Dewey,** and if you're going to use these names, don't forget that William was the brother of Henry, the novelist.

This brings us to the end of the historical section of this inquiry. Twentieth-century philosophers will be treated in a later section (with a little more care; some of them are still alive and thus able to sue).

DEATHS OF THE PHILOSOPHERS

So much for the lives of the philosophers. According to the **Epicureans,** death should mean nothing to us — but in spite of their opinion, we include the following list of bizarre philosophical deaths for the sake of completeness.

Empedocles. There are two traditions about Empedocles' death. According to one, he died of a broken leg; the other says that he jumped into the crater of Mount Etna in order to prove that he was a god. How this was supposed to constitute proof is not recorded.

Heraclitus contracted dropsy as a result of living off grass and plants on a mountainside during a long mood of misanthropy. When doctors told him that his condition was incurable, he undertook his own treatment, prescribing that he be covered from head to foot in manure, then left outdoors (or perhaps it was just that no one would allow him indoors). According to the historian Diogenes Laertius, "He was unable to tear the dung off, and, being unrecognizable, he was devoured by dogs."

Don't mention **Socrates'** death from hemlock in an Athenian jail; everyone knows about it. If you're unlucky enough to have some dullard mention it to you, point out that the description of his death in Plato's *Phaedo* is *entirely* inconsistent with the known effects of hemlock. Tell him "*Some*one was lying—or there was a cover-up," and then smirk.

Pythagoras was a victim of his own extreme vegetarianism. Being pursued by several disenchanted followers, he came to a field of beans, and, rather than trample the beans down, he stayed where he was and was killed.

Crinis the Stoic (a disciple of a philosophy known for its absolute imperturbability and its total indifference to worldly fears) died of fright when a mouse squeaked at him. This is true, and Stoic philosophy has never been taken seriously since.

Chrysippus the Stoic, on the other hand, died laughing at one of his own jokes. An old woman's ass, so the story goes, once ate an enormous basket of Chrysippus's figs, whereupon he offered the woman his wineskin, saying: "Better give him a big swig of this to wash them down with." Then he har-har-ed so hard that he fell down—dead as a doornail. With a sense of humor like that, it's a blessing that only fragments of his 700 books survive. (Let's face it, it's unlikely he'd ever have been booked as a standup comic at the Comedy Store or the Improv.)

Diogenes is supposed to have died in one of three ways:

(1) By forgetting to breathe.
(2) From severe indigestion as a result of eating raw turtle eggs.
(3) From being bitten on the foot while dividing a raw octopus among his dogs.

After the ancient period, the quality of philosophical deaths falls off considerably, although it's perhaps worth recording that **Aquinas** died sitting on the john,

as did **Epicurus** before him. (This may have been more common than it seems considering how much time philosophers probably spent at this particular activity.) **Francis Bacon** died as a result of pneumonia caught while trying to stuff a chicken with snow on Hampstead Heath. He's probably the only person ever to die from researching the ins and outs of fast food, as opposed to dying from actually eating it.

And finally, it was **René Descartes'** misfortune to die of getting up too early in the morning. Reluctantly accepting an invitation to the court of Queen Christina of Sweden, he discovered to his horror that she wanted daily "tutoring," and the only time she wanted it was five o'clock in the morning. The strain killed him.

THE BASIC QUESTIONS
OF PHILOSOPHY

Even if you're only a bluffer-philosopher, you should know a little about **Ontology**, which is the study of What There Is, and you should know something about **Epistemology**, the study of How We Come To Know About It. These words can be used in a variety of ways, but learn a few basic rules to avoid getting into difficulty. The more advanced bluffer can make up his or her own terms.

Epistemology is often linked with the names of individual philosophers, as in "Plato's epistemology" or "Kant's epistemology," although you have to be *very* careful about committing yourself, especially in regard to **Kant,** or any other German philosopher, for that matter.

Ontology is less frequently ascribed to individuals, so be careful—unless you're absolutely sure that the person you're talking to is more ignorant than you are. In bluffing philosophy, this is generally a safe assumption. Take heed. Mistakes can be made, and they can prove costly. Ontologies, however, can be more or less rich: in simple terms, the richer the ontology, the more things there are supposed to be.

Quine (Willard van Orman Quine. Always refer to him as "Quine," or, if very sure of yourself, "Van"). Quine once observed that all the important questions of philosophy were asked regularly by four-year-old children. They are:

(1) What is there? (ontology)
(2) How do you know? (epistemology)
(3) Why should I? (a matter of ethics)

Children don't really get into **Metaphysics** (*q.v.*), which is probably a good thing. But the most common and irritating question that *all* children ask is "Why?" — the Basic Question of Philosophy.

Levels and Meta-Levels

"Meta" is a word (or rather a prefix) that's absolutely essential to the ambitious bluffer. Its use originates with the invention of **Metaphysics** by Aristotle. The literal meaning of "meta" in Greek is "with" or "after," and Aristotle's "Metaphysics" were the things that seemed to be beyond the scope of Physics. It's sometimes said that they were called that because they contained Truths at a deeper, more arcane, more fundamental level than could be found in Physics. This is nonsense. The truth is that in the standard early edition of Aristotle (done by one Andronicus of Rhodes), the *Metaphysics* came out in the volumes immediately *subsequent* to those which contained the *Physics.* As a result of that historical accident, combined with the fact that no one could come up with any suitable, alternate name for the philosophical grab bag of logic, theology, epistemology, and mathematics that constitutes Aristotle's *Metaphysics,* the term "meta" has come to signify any study at a deeper level than the study following the prefix.

So, if you do meta-mathematics, and our advice is not to, you'll study *not* the theorems and proofs of math itself, but the basis for accepting them and the Formal Structure they exemplify. Meta-ethics, similarly, is not the study of what we *ought* to do, but the study of the *nature* of the theories that tell us what we ought to do.

It will be clear that, properly deployed, "meta" is a tool of devasting conversational force.

A meta-language is a language in which you discuss the structure of another language, known as the object-language. You might try remarking that the object language is often contained in the meta-language but never vice versa; don't bother about what that means. Thus, the last clause, in which we discussed meta-language, was in fact an example of meta-language, and that last sentence . . . well, you get the general idea. (It's all beginning to make sense now, isn't it? Aren't you glad now you decided to pick up this little bluffer's friend rather than that new issue of *Playboy* or *Playgirl*? Can you say "meta-physics"? We *knew* you could.)

There's an opportunity here to go into **Infinite Regress,** the philosophical equivalent of banging your head against a brick wall. **Alfred Tarski,** a logician of the inter-war years, when all logicians seemed to be Polish (though not, of course, vice versa), actually believed that only by positing a theoretically infinite hierarchy of languages could we fully explicate (a good bluffer's word) the notion of truth as it functions in ordinary language. The reasons for this are extremely complex and difficult and can be mastered only after *years* of study. Say so.

Equally difficult to understand is the American philosopher **Donald Davidson,** who started off as a theoretical psychologist, but found that it was much too easy and became a philosopher instead. He adapted and expanded Tarski's theories in an attempt to supply philosophy and natural languages with a Theory of Meaning. You might try wondering politely if Davidson's extension of Tarskian semantics is really viable; but on no account get drawn into a long conversation on the subject.

With a little practice, however, you can easily create your *own* meta-disciplines—and indeed not just disciplines. **G. E. L. Owen** used to refer to his "meta-diary," which was the piece of paper on which he'd written where he'd left his diary. So much for that! Now, on to the Big Meta: metaphysics.

Metaphysics

Metaphysics is about what there *really* is (as opposed to merely what there *is*—which is, of course, ontology), what people in unguarded moments tend to refer to as the Underlying Structure of the World. Put like that, it sounds a little like contemporary particle physics, if less obviously obtuse, but there's a sense in which traditional metaphysics *has* been taken over by modern science. Metaphysics is difficult, but if the **Positivists** are right, it's impossible. It is, in fact, increasingly common to graduate with a degree in philosophy without having the least idea of what metaphysics is. Thus, you, as a bluffer, need to have only the *vaguest* notion of what it's all about—but it's important, as always, to have *strong* opinions about it.

Whether there is a God, or What is the Nature of Substance, or the Structure of Casual Connections, or whether Oral Roberts really would have been "called home" had he not raised x-millions of dollars—all these might be said to be broadly metaphysical questions, which is to say, among other things, that they have no clear answers. This is what the **Logical Positivists,** a collection of Viennese philosophers with silly names, had against the entire field of metaphysics.

When talking about (or even safer yet, simply mentioning) metaphysics, it's best to adopt one of two approaches. You can simply refuse to accept the existence of any such subject (best done with a patronizing smile), in which case the **Positivists** come in handy; or alternately, you can try to make your voice sound as if you were penetrating some exquisitely theoretically ineffable mystery. Bring up "early Wittgenstein." He's ideal for the first purpose; "late Wittgenstein" will do for the latter. In fact, Wittgenstein is always good because almost everyone has heard of him, but almost no one has actually read him—and fewer still can claim with any conviction to have understood him.

With the Positivists, throw around their Principle of Verifiability. This states that we know the meaning of any sentence only if we know what it would take for that sentence to be true. If there's no method of verifying it, at least in principle, then the sentence is meaningless. This approach makes almost all traditional metaphysics, as well as most of what's said by economists and Baptist clergymen, literally meaningless.

Ethics

One of the great pleasures of a philosopher's life is being able to tell everyone (and not just children and

small dogs) what they ought to do. This is **Ethics.**
Speaking generally, and you will be, there are basically
two types of Ethical Theory. You can be either a **Con-
sequentialist** or a **Deontologist.**

Consequentialists believe that the moral quality of
actions is determined solely by their results. **Deontologists,** on the other hand, believe that there are
some things that one *ought* to do, and other things that
one should *refrain* from doing—irrespective of what the
actual or probable results of that action are. The most
famous version of consequentialism is **Utilitarianism,**
classically articulated by **Bentham** and **Mill** in the last
century, and it's still alive and kicking.

The classical form of the Utilitarian ethic holds that
one should act so as to produce the greatest good for
the greatest number. How that good is defined, and
by whom, what to do in the case of incompatible
goods, whether the total number of people involved
matters or not, and if so how, are only *some* of the
initial problems with interpreting the doctrine.

The principal trouble with Utilitarianism, or rather
any variety of it (it comes in a number of flavors), is
that it gives rise, in problem cases, to "counter-intuitive"
results. Try out the following ploy with someone who
claims to be a Utilitarian. Suppose you have three people, each suffering from a terminal collapse of one of
their vital organs, whereas you, on the other hand, are
as healthy as a horse. As a Utilitarian, you would have
to consent to being hauled off to the hospital and cut
open to transplant your healthy organs into the bodies
of your ailing friends, ensuring a net gain of two lives.
Anti-utilitarians feel that, not implausibly, you might
not be too happy with this credo.

The advantage of Utilitarianism is that, at least in its basic idea, it's fairly straightforward, although it's been objected that if you take the idea of consequentialisms seriously, you'd spend your whole lifetime trying to calculate the precise effect of any action and thus end up doing nothing at all. It's generally *not* a good idea to claim that this is, in itself, an advantage of the theory.

Deontologists, by contrast, are a lot more troublesome. The obvious difficulty consists in spelling out just what the duties and concomitant rights actually are. There's very little consensus on this, and it gets us into the **Subjectivist/Objectivist** debate: are morals discovered, as the Objectivist likes to think, by some peculiar faculty, or are they matters of convenience, created in a more or less arbitrary way in order to make social (and most forms of anti-social) activity possible? It's a good idea to have a view on this.

If you decide to take up Subjectivism, you should be aware that it's likely to commit you, unless you contrive some pretty fancy footwork, to **Cultural Relativism,** a stance not without its own set of dangers. A Cultural Relativist holds that no one society has the right to say what's right or wrong about any other one, which takes a good deal of fun out of life, as well as making international relations, as currently practiced by the Bush administration, an impossibility. This entails that, while infanticide and infibulation may be a little bit out of order in Itta Bena, Mississippi, they may be perfectly okay in Pignon, Haiti. This can get you in serious difficulties, particularly with some of today's feminists.

Perhaps the best line to take is that adopted by **Dick**

Hare (a philosopher, not a genital complaint), who remarked that he'd never been able to understand what was supposed to be the difference between the two stances. Then he added, with a dash of bravado, that he'd never met anyone else who could either. This is a brilliant example of one of the advanced bluffer's most useful techniques: to pretend that the blindingly obvious is, in fact, hopelessly obscure. It's just that lesser minds can't appreciate its inherent complexity. Wittgenstein employed this method from time to time, but Hare is the master. Once he even claimed that he didn't really understand the meaning of the word "it."

Whatever your thoughts are on the Origin of Morals, you should have a few facts in your back pocket about moral theory—which brings us back to **Deontologies.** For classical versions, **Kant** is the name to finesse with, especially with his famous **Categorical Imperative.** This has several different formulations in his work, which is good news for the bluffer: "Yes, but *which* version of Kant's Principle did you have in mind?" has been known to work like a charm. The principle, very briefly, if obscurely, can be expressed as follows:

> Act only according to that maxim by which you can at the same time will that it should become a general law.

This is generally interpreted to mean that you should do *only* the kind of things you wouldn't mind everybody *else* doing. Right away, it's clear that there are difficulties with this. You might like to take a nap, but you wouldn't care for the rest of the world joining you in the same bed.

The principal advocates of deontologies these days are the churches and some factions of the K.K.K.

Philosophers are, for the most part, at least in their personal lives, an amoral bunch of alley cats (this is particularly true of moral philosophers). They tend to think less in terms of duties than of rights and tend to create **Rights Theories.** You have a Right *only* if it's something you should be allowed to get away with.

An important principle of most Rights Theories is that of "Universalisability," which is, because of its length, an excellent word to use now and then. It means that you or I have a right *only* if everyone else has a similar right. So, if you buy a Rights Theory along with Universalisability, you have to be pretty careful about what rights you claim to have — in case some other clown gets his hands on them.

Nonetheless, rights are good bluffing fodder. For a start, almost everybody who thinks they have rights at all hold inconsistent beliefs about them (for instance, everyone has the right to life, yet the oppressed have a right to kill tyrants), and it usually requires only a little ingenuity to discover and exploit these inconsistencies. This will give you a great feeling of intellectual superiority and leave your adversary nursing a strong desire to kick ass — which is, after all, what it's all about.

The drawback, of course, is that you yourself may be accused of holding an Inconsistent Set of Principles. If this happens, you should confess right away that the principles you've been trapped into admitting were not *meant* to be *un*qualified; in other words, there are exceptions that prove the rule — whatever that means. In certain specifiable circumstances (try to avoid having to specify them), one will take precedence over another. Your set of principles, you say earnestly, is hierarchic. Then point out gravely that it's all a matter of systematizing your moral science.

Another useful technical distinction to draw is between Act-centered and Agent-centered theories of ethics. As you might guess, this is all about What Really Matters: the sorts of thing we do or the kinds of people we are (for we all know that the most appalling social piranhas can, on occasion, do things we approve of, even lawyers). Of course, any sensible theory is neither exclusively one thing or the other, and it's generally safe to say something to that effect without fear of having to say just how much of one or the exact proportion of the other. Another useful gambit is: "Don't you think that presupposes an excessively act-centered (or agent-centered, as the case may be) view of morality?"

As a general rule, it's advisable to have a set of unorthodox (and infuriating) views, particularly on the so-called New Moral Problems, if indeed they're new at all. NMPs are difficulties generated by such advances as test-tube babies, surrogacy, fetal experimentation, and the like. The possibility of large-scale cloning is another, if potential, NMP. Euthanasia, which has been practiced in one form or another since the emergence of the human race, is for some reason frequently considered an NMP. Be suitably dismissive about this. There's a customary distinction between active and passive euthanasia. The former is actually killing, the latter merely letting die. Try arguing that this distinction is spurious: "After all, the doctor who refuses treatment *intends* the patient to die, and he has the means to prolong life. By his negligence he's just as responsible for the patient's death as if he took a meat cleaver to him." A subtle variation of this is to say that passive euthanasia is actually *more* immoral than the active sort, which can, after all, be carried out in a humane and painless way; whereas with the former, you effectively ensure that the patient dies in extreme pain. This argument is particularly effective with doctors – it enrages them, and the world holds few sweeter sights than a hopping-mad physician.

As for other moral problems, new, middle-aged, or ancient, our advice is to cut your cloth to suit the occasion. If confronting a feminist about abortion, or any question involving Fetal Rights, you might politely inquire if a Woman's Right to Choose extends to a Right to Choose to Kill. You need to be prepared for this, and have good reasons for thinking fetuses have rights; it isn't good enough to be a Catholic – Bentham's view that the ability to suffer pain confers rights may come in handy.

This is an area that rewards argumentative inventiveness. It's not without risks, but it can pay rich dividends. Find a moral position, fortify it with suitable arguments (they don't have to be *sound*, but it does help if they're *valid* – see Glossary for this important distinction), and you're off. For instance, you can argue that marriage is immoral. This is surprisingly easy, and can be delightfully irritating, particularly to newlyweds and their parents – but we leave you to work out the details. Bluffing is a creative activity.

Logic

This is an important branch of philosophical enquiry. **Logic,** as a formal study, is fiendishly difficult, and the best thing to do is Leave It Alone. All you really need to know is that it was all right when everyone was into

Aristotelian Syllogisms, but it got all fouled up in the last century by the development of mathematical logic, in particular by **Gottlob Frege** (an *excellent* name to drop, even if he was an anti-Semetic proto-fascist), **Russell,** and **Whitehead** (*q.v.*). The new logic offered a thesaurus of possibles (technically it can deal with the logic of relations; relations between things, that is, not the warped logic of your father-in-law).

Things got worse with the development of **Alternative Logic** (sometimes campily referred to as **Deviant Logic**). These increase the number of truth-values and question the validity of certain traditional logical laws, such as the **Law of the Excluded Middle,** which says (roughly) that everything either *is* something or it *isn't*. Under no circumstances commit yourself on this.

In addition to **Formal Logic** and, of course, **Meta-Logic,** there's **Philosophical Logic.** Like many things, this should be discussed in a veddy, veddy prissy British accent: try it and see. It's a large and confusing area — rather like London and John Maynard Keynes, and, also like John Maynard and London's Soho at Night, it should be given a wide berth. You might like to know that one of its central concerns is **Theory of Meaning.** You might comment sadly that none of the available semantic theories on the market seems very satisfactory, but on no account try to explain why. It's usually safe to adopt this line, because one of the pervasive features of philosophy is that nothing in it is ever entirely satisfactory.

Epistemology

Almost all you really need to know about **epistemol-**

ogy is how to spell it. However, a remark like "But how can we *know* that we know that?" is effective at times but shouldn't be overdone.

Philosophy of Religion

Like most things in philosophy, this is much better as a destructive pursuit that it is as a constructive pursuit. People with strong religious views are excellent meat for the good philosophical bluffer; while they're usually sensitive and can be deeply hurt by what you say, they're invariably too polite to say so.

If you don't want to get embroiled in the issue of whether God exists, or if so, what he thinks he's doing, the best thing to do is to steer the conversation towards the Problem of Evil. If God loves us and the world, why are *we* and *it* so goddamned screwed up?

An elegantly beautiful version of this argument was supplied by **Lactantius**:

> Given that there is evil (while bearing in mind the supposed attributes of God), then either (1) God knows about evil, cares about it, but can't do anything about it; or (2) He would care about it, could do something about it, but doesn't know about it; or (3) He knows about it, could do something about it, but doesn't care about it.

Philosophy of Science

As philosophy is essentially a meta-activity, there can be philosophies of just about anything, and science is no exception. How do scientists develop theories? What is the relation between theory and evidence? What is the experimental method? How does one theory gain ascendancy over another without money changing hands? These, and similar questions, are the province of the **Philosophy of Science,** which has enjoyed a boom of popularity in the last fifty years or so, partly because it gives philosophers the unfamiliar sensation that what they're doing is of some relevance to something – and partly because it's yet another area in which they have the pleasure of telling people where to get off.

Karl Popper (love that name!) figured prominently in the development of the recent debates, with his view that theories can never be verified (proved true); they can only be refuted (shown to be full of sound and fury and signifying nothing). The reason for this is that no amount of empirical evidence will ever show beyond all doubt that the world will continue to behave in the way it's always been observed to; whereas one bad result, such as water boiling at fifty degrees or an edible airline omelet, can refute an entire theory. The reason for *this,* according to Popper, is that proper theories are made up of exceptionless generalizations universally quantified, or, more intelligibly, they consist of sentences like "All somethings are something else." According to Popper, science progresses by means of **Bold Conjectures** ("The world is made entirely of cheese") followed by **Conclusive Refutations** ("It can't be: mice absolutely *loathe* it"). The trouble with this as a view is that, generally speaking, the bolder the conjecture, the more obviously nutty it is.

Various people have offered all kinds of different oddball names to drop. A particularly good name to drop is **T. S. Kuhn,** who salivates over Scientific Revolutions, which involve what he calls **Paradigm Shifts.** This idea is extraordinarily difficult to pin down, and for that reason it's terrifically invaluable. In its most general terms, it means that people just decide to stop looking at the world in one way and start looking at it in another. So feel free to throw in T. S. Kuhn if you're ever caught between a conversational rock and a philosophical hard place. Meanwhile, back to Popper.

Hilary Putnam (philosophers of science don't all have silly names, they just seem to) mused that if Popper is right, *no* theory is refutable, for no theory, just like no man, is an island. So there you are. Yet another scientific philosopher brings up **Auxiliary Assumptions** about the nature of the universe and presents you with an **Anomaly.** You have a choice; throw out either the theory or an **Auxiliary Assumption** – or both, if you're feeling extravagant.

Other names to drop are **Imre Lakatos** if you can pronounce it, and **Paul Feyerabend,** a self-confessed methodological anarchist, who urged scientists to adopt as their research motto "anything goes." In addition to his having imported Cole Porter into philosophy, something no one else has ever managed to do, Feyerabend was a notable eccentric: he used to end his lectures at the London School of Economics by leaping out an open (fortunately, first floor) window, onto a motorcycle, and roaring off into the sunset.

THE CONTEMPORARY SCENE

The Anglo-Saxon Philosophers

Anglo-Saxon philosophers (including the Finns, of course) tend to deny that they're part of any particular philosopical school or sect; indeed, they're apt to label philosophical sectarianism as a dangerous Continental habit and, consequently, one to be despised. Like overweight lovers in the tropics, they do tend to stick together, as if seeking safety in numbers and perhaps believing, possibly correctly, that they need it.

Before World War I, the two most important figures in British philosophy were probably (remember, don't commit yourself if you can avoid it) **Bertrand Russell** and **G. E. Moore.** Russell made his reputation with the publication of *Principia Mathematica,* co-written with **E. A. Whitehead.** Sometimes the book is referred to as "Russell and Whitehead," much in the same vein as we say "Masters and Johnson." It's an extremely detailed exposition of formal symbolic logic, and, as such, *not* recommended reading material for commuters. In fact, we don't recommend it as reading material at all.

Moore, not to be outdone as far as pretentious-sounding Latinate titles were concerned, immediately cranked out his *Principia Ethica,* a treatise on moral philosophy, in which he said that "good" was inde-finable but *was* the name of a "non-natural quality." A conception of Moore's much discussed in this context is that of the **Naturalistic Fallacy.** It's hard to say *exactly* what this is. Moore's idea seems to be that you can't define ethical terms in terms of non-ethical ones, and you can't deduce ethical propositions from factual, non-ethical ones. Got it?

This ambiguity makes the Naturalistic Fallacy extremely useful, particularly if you never argue why it's a fallacy, but simply assert that it *is* one. You can supplement this in conversation usefully with another concept of Moore's, the **Open Question Argument.** This means that no matter what is factually true for some particular object or property (that people like it, for instance; or that it's cheese-flavored), it's still an **Open Question** whether or not it's "good." Moore was renowned for his square-shouldered, no-nonsense approach to philosophy. He once told an astonished audience that nothing was certain — except the fact that he had two hands. It's not clear who had been disposed to doubt it.

As for Russell, his other major contributions to phi-losophy, as opposed to his other major concerns, which included pacifism and promiscuity (he liked both) and can be summed up by the sixties slogan "Make love, not war" (which Russell did to an enviably old age), include the discovery of **Russell's Paradox,** which knocked the stuffing out of the naive **Set-Theory** and the **Theory of Descriptions.**

The **Theory of Descriptions** tries to analyze the logic of natural language (remember this phrase) and, in particular, the problem of **Proper Names.** This, like most philosophical problems, isn't a problem to anyone who isn't a philosopher. Russell usually quoted such sentences as "The present King of France is bald" or "Scott wrote the Waverley novels." The latter, according to Russell, actually means that "someone wrote the Waverley novels, only one person wrote the Waverley novels, and if anyone wrote the Waverley novels, that person was Scott." From this, one can be tempted to deduce that philosophers know as much about ordinary language as they do about ordinary people (see Introduction).

Concerning Russell's best-selling *History of Western Philosophy*, praise its style, "lucidity," and humor, but (and pause here) say that you have reservations about its actual content: "Well written, of course, but sort of a lopsided interpretation, don't you think?" "Don't you think?" is a rhetorical question and should never be taken literally.

Perhaps the most influential philosophical meeting (before World War I) occurred in 1912, when the (Very) Early **Wittgenstein** met Russell in Cambridge and asked him (Russell) if he (the Very Early Wittgenstein) was a complete idiot—because if he was, he (the Very Early Wittgenstein) was going to become an airplane pilot. Russell told him to go away and write something. The Very Early Wittgenstein did so. Russell read one line of it and told him he was far too bright to be a pilot. The war interrupted the Very Early Wittgenstein's career in Cambridge, but he returned afterward as the Early Wittgenstein and proceeded to dominate philosophical life in Cambridge (and elsewhere) for the next thirty years.

A fascinatingly eccentric man with a passion for

god-awful movies, the Early Wittgenstein virtually lived in a deck chair under an electric fan in an otherwise bare room in Trinity College at Cambridge. Oddly enough, he published only one book in his lifetime, the *Tractatus Logico-Philosophicus,* in which he tackled such problems as the structure of the proposition, how language is meaningful, and the concept of truth. His research led him to believe that only propositions built from basic atomic propositions with logical connectives were meaningful. Hence, the name **Logical Atomism** for this type of philosophy. Everything else was literally meaningless, so this gets rid of metaphysics, along with a lot of other junk. In fact, it has the unfortunate consequence of making almost all of the *Tractatus* itself — if true — meaningless. Even the Early Wittgenstein himself acknowledged this, saying that only if in some sense you already knew what he meant, would you be able to understand his writings. He added that his philosophy was like a ladder which you threw away after climbing it. Many people took his metaphor literally. The last sentence of the book sums it up: "Whereof one cannot speak, thereof there must be silence." The really ambitious bluffer can state it emphatically in German: "Wovon man nicht sprechen kann, darüber muss man schweigen."

The Early Wittgenstein then gave up philosophy for a while, thinking that he'd said it all. Later he changed his mind. This is the crucial point at which the Early Wittgenstein becomes the Later Wittgenstein, and, as such, he becomes the second truly influential figure in philosophy between the wars (after the Early Wittgenstein).

In his *Tractatus,* the Early Wittgenstein had said that

propositions had meaning because they were like pictures of the facts they referred to. The Later Wittgenstein disagreed, arguing that ordinary language was both more complex and more meaningful than the Early Wittgenstein had given it credit. The posthumous result of this is the *Philosophical Investigations*. The Late Wittgenstein died in 1951, and, ever since, there's been a steady stream of posthumously published notebooks, lectures, laundry lists, notes to his landlady, etc., giving him the remarkable distinction of having written one book during his lifetime but about fifteen after his death.

After the War, English philosophy centered around Oxford, although Cambridge would disagree, and a mysterious entity known as **Oxford Philosophy** (or more derisively, **Linguistic Philosophy**) came into existence. Its chief exponents were **Gilbert Ryle**, a renowned pipe smoker, and **J. L. Austin**, another renowned pipe smoker. Austin was well known for his "Saturday mornings," during which a group of distinguished philosophers, distinguished principally by the fact that they all smoked pipes, would get together to discuss the subtle nuances of ordinary language — or splitting hairs, depending on your point of view. This tended to take the form of distinguishing six different meanings of words like "wheelbarrow" and, not surprisingly, provoked anger or derision among those who were excluded for whatever reason — such as not being bright enough or not smoking a pipe.

However, it's generally accepted (except, of course, in Oxford) that since the War, the center of gravity of Anglo-Saxon philosophy has shifted to Uncle Sam's shores (even the Finnish bit), a state of affairs which may not be totally unrelated to the fact that U.S. universities pay enormous salaries (even though most of them go to athletic coaches).

The Grand Old Man of American philosophy is **Willard van Orman Quine** ("Van" to his buddies), who is memorable for believing that Kant's distinction between analytic and synthetic (see Glossary) is at best vague and at worst useless and for having called a book of his *From a Logical Point of View*, after a Harry Belafonte calypso song.

His successors include **Saul Kripke,** in the field of philosophical logic and the study of **Modality** (don't worry about what that is). His major work, *Naming and Necessity,* is about **Proper Names, Sense and Reference, Possible Worlds,** and many other terms you'll find at the end of the book. It's worth mentioning in passing because it's probably the most significant piece of philosophical work done since the War.

You'll score points if you point out that in American philosophy, the Oddball Name is as great an asset as it was to the **Viennese Positivists,** many of whom ended up in America—perhaps for this very reason. This was confirmed by **Alvin Plantinga,** a modal logician and philosopher of religion (potentially a lethal combination), and **Robert Nozick,** a radical right-wing political anarchist who thinks that everything should be privatized.

Another American philosopher of importance is **John Rawls,** whose major book, *A Theory of Justice,* was a popular and critical success. Basically, Rawls holds that justice can be defined by two principles:

(1) Everyone should have the same freedom as

everyone else, and, given that constraint, as much freedom as possible.

(2) Economic inequalities between people are justified only if those who are worse off are, in fact, better off under this arrangement than they would be under another, more equal one.

Be careful with this. It isn't as silly as it seems at first, but it does allow for extreme inequalities of goods, which may be held to count against the system — unless, of course, you stand to benefit from them. This type of thing is known as a **Theory of Distributive Justice** and can come in handy. (Particularly if you're interested in robbing the poor and giving to the rich — more commonly known as Classic Reaganomics.)

The Continentals

The **Continentals** come in two main varieties, the French and the Germans.

Perhaps the most important Continental philosophical movement of recent times has been **Existentialism,** which has had both French and German adherents. The principal French exponent was **Sartre,** who combined philosophy with vigorous Marxist politics, wrote novels and plays, and had a prodigious capacity for booze. He coined the slogan "existence precedes essence," which means that we should be less concerned with what *type* of things things are than with the fact that they simply *are.* **Existentialists** resist classification, tending to insist on the autonomy of the individual. For that reason, they tend to get a little teed-off about being called Existentialists at all.

Existentialism, at least the French variety of it, has strong literary connections, **Camus** and Sartre himself being the most important exponents. Their literature tends to focus on the concept of the *acte gratuit*, or gratuitous action (refer to it in French, or course), which is supposed to be the essence of the Existentialist's affirmation of his own existence. To outsiders, it generally seems more like self-centered amusement at someone else's expense. As the *acte gratuit*, at least in literature, tends to be a violent, or, at the very least, an anti-social act, life with an Existentialist (at least a French one) is more than a little hard on the nerves.

The German Existentialists **Martin Heidegger** and **Karl Jaspers,** in particular, are a different bunch. They had no pretensions to literary excellence, luckily, and tend to be more explicit about their debt to earlier philosophers, such as **Kierkegaard** and **Edmund Husserl,** a turn-of-the-century German who developed a systematic and thoroughly Teutonic concept of **Phenomenology**—that is, the attempt to penetrate below the surface of the appearances of things to the basic reality of our conscious apprehensions of them (or something).

Existentialism carries no inherent religious commitment. Sartre was an atheist, Jaspers a Christian, Heidegger a Nazi, but this is generally (conveniently) forgotten. An interesting point to note is that whereas books of philosophy written in English generally have to have three elements to their titles—*Language, Truth, and Logic; Truth, Probability, and Paradox; Mind, Language, and Reality; Sex, Drugs, and Rock 'n Roll,* being some prominent examples—the requisite number for Existentialist titles seems to be two, as in Heidegger's

Sein und Zeit (Being and Time) and Sartre's *L'Être et Néant (Being and Nothingness)*. Anglo-Saxon analytic philosophers are inclined to despise Existentialism for not been sufficiently analytic. By the same token, Existentialists are inclined to despise Anglo-Saxon analytic philosophers for simply not being sufficiently *anything*.

Enough has been said elsewhere in this book about **Logical Positivism.** It's enough just to remember that its exponents are closely linked with the Anglo-Saxon tradition. Many of them fled Europe and Hitler in the thirties for America, where **Rudolph Carnap** and **Carl Hempel** have been particularly influential since the War, particularly in the philosophy of science. The most important of the English Logical Positivists (which, incidentally, include the Early but not the Late Wittgenstein) was **A. J. Ayer,** who is still perhaps best known for his first book, *Language, Truth, and Logic,* even though he no longer believes much of what it contains.

Finally, there are two important elements of modern Continental thought which have not been mentioned so far. These are **Structuralism** and its rather shadowy successor, **Post-Structuralism.**

Structuralism orginally began as a method in linguistics with **Saussure** and penetrated anthropology with **Levi-Strauss,** at least in France and in the English Literature departments of American universities. Almost no one will admit to being a Structuralist, and it's hard to say exactly what Structuralists *are.* However, it's important to have strong views about them. They're almost universally ignored in British philosophy departments, which demonstrates the rigorous analytically preoccupation of British philosophy—or its appalling insularity, depending on which side you're on. (Make sure you're on one, but only one.)

Two key characteristics of Structuralism and Post-Structuralism are their distrust of academic disciplines and their impenetrable jargon. Leading exponents include **Roland Barthes** (in the field of literary criticism and its social ramifications), **Michel Foucault** (history, sociology, and sex), and **Jacques Derrida** (language, literary criticism, rhetoric). The latter is in many ways, the most interesting, if also the most obscure. Opinions vary widely as to his stature — thinker, genius, or charlatan, according to your taste. Derrida has particularly annoyed analytic philosophers (Anglo-Saxon ones, that is), at least those who've bothered to read any of his stuff, because he tries to show that beneath its carefully cultivated surface of logic, analysis, and objective inquiry, analytic philosophy is a highly biased, subjective business. He uses a method known as **Deconstructionism,** which is in danger of becoming a major industry in North America and is essentially the enterprise of showing that some literary work or other generates within itself fatal contradictions and incoherencies which undermine the argument that it ostensibly advances.

Perhaps the safest course to take with the modern Continentals is:

(1) claim that what they say is literally meaningless,
(2) follow the analytic philosopher's line and say that whatever is it, it isn't philosophy, or
(3) remark cautiously that it shouldn't be dismissed *too* hastily.

This last ploy is best done to someone holding one of the other two views.

SOME USEFUL TECHNIQUES

This section is a brief guide to some of the more important, basic arts of the philosophical bluffer.

1. The Question

It's always a good idea to phrase your remarks in the form of a question, particularly if you've no idea of what you're talking about, as happens about 85 percent of the time in philosophy. Thus say, "Don't you suppose that presupposes some rather implausible assumptions?" rather than "That presupposes some implausible assumptions."

2. The Hedge

Never *ever* commit yourself. If it's possible to hedge, and it nearly always is in philosophy, hedge. Cover your you-know-what. Leave yourself escape routes. An incidental advantage of this procedure is to confer upon the bluffer an air of appropriate intellectual caution. Statements like "It seems to me, at least" (when it doesn't), or "I'm inclined to think that" (even when you aren't), and "Perhaps there's something to be said for it" (particularly when there obviously isn't). These should be used over and over. The really expert philosophical bluffer will *never* say anything that he or she can't quietly and unobtrusively retract if the need arises. In this respect, philosophical bluffers closely resemble professional philosophers.

3. Delivery

It's important to make your remarks in the right tone of voice; your delivery should be slow, measured, and thoughtful. Try to give the impression that everything you say has been carefully thought out. As a result, you'll find that even a mouthful of non sequiturs will sound intelligent and profound.

4. Appearance

Many otherwise competent bluffers lose valuable points for not paying sufficient attention to this point. Generally speaking, there are two types of philosophers:

(1) the precise, neat, impeccably dressed Nietzschian Superman, and
(2) the unbelievably scruffy, smelly, absent-minded Bum.

The latter is perhaps the more common, but the former is by no means unknown, and a suave, cool, controlled manner can pay rich dividends. On the other hand, Charles Bukowski's type of extraordinary eccentricity is surprisingly difficult to carry off (unless, of course, you happen to be Mickey Rourke *or* Charles Bukowski.) So, other things being equal, we recommend no. 1 unless you suffer from some crippling personal disqualification, such as the body of Quasimodo and the fashion sense of Bob Goldthwaite. No. 1 is particularly recommended for women. At least, someone may listen to you.

PHILOSOPHER #1

PHILOSOPHER #2

5. Itemization

Philosophy is supposed to be an orderly, logical subject, treating confusing and difficult matters in an orderly, logical way (*ha!*). The truly great bluffer is the one who can give the *impression* of doing this while, in fact, doing exactly the opposite – and the way to do this is through itemization. For example, "That seems to me to raise at least three questions" is a good start, especially if it doesn't raise any at all. The more questions you can raise the better. In general, go for it: three is the minimum, four adequate, and six or even seven have been known to wreak devastating destruction. Trust to luck and ingenuity. In any case, if you come up with enough questions, your adversary will lose count.

6. Props

We're now getting to the advanced stage, and most upper-level bluffers cultivate at least one prop. For men, the most effective and versatile is the pipe. Many genuine philosophers smoke pipes. The reason is self-evident. If you're asked a really tough question, or are otherwise put on the spot, all you have to do is take your pipe out of an inside pocket (you'll find that this makes the inside pocket particularly disgusting after a few days, but bluffers, like everyone else, must suffer for their art). Then make a preliminary remark, such as "Well the *really* important thing about that seems to *me* to be . . ." and then set about lighting your pipe. You can make this operation last five minutes with no difficulty – and much longer with practice – provided you interject the occasional comment of an entirely noncommittal nature as you knock, clean, scrape, blow through, dismantle, reassemble, load, pack, tamp, light, draw on, relight, retamp, draw on again, and produce large and noxious clouds of smoke. No one will suspect that you're playing for time. Do this well enough, and you can avoid having to answer the question at all.

Other props, like offering cigarettes, cleaning glasses, blowing the nose powerfully and lengthily, or even feigning a fit of coughing all have their uses, but none of them beats the pipe, which also manages for some reason to make whoever is smoking it look knowledge-able and philosophical.

7. Language

Select a few examples of choice jargon that you like the sound of—then flog them to death. And remember the Golden Rule: never say anything in English if you can say it in some other language (preferably German).

8. Playing for Time

It's never out of order to remark, with an air of deep seriousness, that you'll have to give the matter more thought. This is doubly effective. It does away with the obligation to say anything that might commit you to something, and it tends to make your adversary feel intellectually inferior. This is particularly true if the matter in question is, in fact, something ridiculously obvious. Remember to always strive to complicate whatever is essentially simple.

9. Pretense of Profundity

This is closely related, of course (note that "of course"), and properly deployed, it's a powerful weapon of conversational power for the previous technique. "It's

much more difficult than most people give it credit for"
is a great phrase to use in a crisis.

10. Invention

If you're ever in a tight spot, with no possible way
out, don't underestimate the power of sheer, inspired
invention. Somebody once remarked that there's no
position or doctrine so absurd that it hasn't at some
time been held by some philosopher or other. Using
this as your cue, feel free to invent philosophers at will.
Ideas for this plot involve little-known, nineteenth-
century German metaphysicians. You could make use
of Heinrich Niemand, Professor of the Philosophy of
Dairy Produce at the University of Bad Homburg, a
wonderous man, who, in addition to having the virtue
of never actually existing, gets you out of all kinds of
difficulties. "Well, it may *sound* bizarre, but Niemand
said it," you say on these occasions, and generally, it
works like a charm.

What Philosophy Isn't

A common misconception is that philosophy is
similiar to religion. A good line to take when someone
drops this clinker is to observe that philosophy is concerned with undermining and questioning dogmas,
whereas religion is obsessed with accepting and sup-
porting them.

You'll also probably meet people (if you're not careful)
who claim to be interested in something called "Eastern
Philosophy," or "Oriental Mysticism." There's only one
thing to do when confronted by this sort of person.
Point out firmly that whatever Eastern Philosophy or

Oriental Mysticism is, it *isn't* philosophy. Be firm about this. This is not to underestimate the practitioners of Ouija board baloney, of course. Some people can carry this off extremely well, and there's lots of mileage to be made in mysticism.

Footnote: How To Be a Mystic

(1) Invent a few meaningless paradoxes (such as "The only true light in the darkness" or "Each step forward is a step backward").

(2) Throw out some pointless proverbs (like "He who talks with the goldfish is lucky to receive an answer" or "The taller the tree, the thinner the fruit").

(3) Profess a belief in at least one metaphysical absurdity, such as Everything is All One or Ordinary Reality is Merely a Base Illusion in Comparison with the True Light of the Godhead. Remember to talk in Capital Letters.

(4) Suggest in an obscure way that the Road to Enlightenment, although Long and Hard, is Ultimately Traversable, and hint that a good method of traversing it is by entering into a Close Personal Relationship with Yourself (or your Guru).

(5) At all times, wear a Benign Smile; for practical purposes, this is virtually indistinguishable from the Insane Grin.

GLOSSARY

Remember the Bluffer's Golden Rule: things always sound better in languages people don't understand. This is particularly true, for some reason, of German. Thus:

Zeitgeist—The Spirit of the Age, the general prevailing viewpoint of mankind at any particular time (if any).

Weltanschauung—(This is a word to take your hat off to.) View of the World; World Picture. Experiment with remarks like "It's the kind of thing that forces one to change one's Weltanschauung."

Erkenntnis—Knowledge; also the name of the journal of the Viennese Logical Positivists (men like Otto Neurath, Carl Hempel, and Rudolph Carnap), who were known as

Der Wiener Kreis—The Vienna Circle.

Sinn und Bedeutung—Sense and Significance, a distinction between two sorts of signification made by Frege (*q.v.*), and one of the cornerstones of modern philosophical logic.

Gesamtheit—Totality; useful in Wittgenstein's dictum "Die Welt is die Gesamtheit der Tatsachen, nicht der Dinge" (The world is the totality of facts, not things). Not to be confused with "Gesundheit."

But you can't get away with German all the time. You must somehow come to grips (however tenuous) with some terms in English.

Logic — A very useful word. It can designate either a formal system of reasoning (like Aristotelian Syllogistic Logic), or it can be used (loosely) to indicate the argumentative force of a piece of reasoning. "What is the *logic* of that argument?" is a useful question to ask — particularly if you need time to get out of a tight spot.

Argument — In the philosophical vocabulary, a reasoned exposition of a point of view — not as in ordinary language, a verbal knock-down drag-out (though it's surprising how often one degenerates into the other). An argument can be either *valid* or *invalid, sound* or *unsound.* An argument is *valid* if it consists of premises linked in such a way that, if they are true, then the conclusion drawn from them is true. It's *sound* only if all the premises are true, and it's valid as well (thus ensuring the truth of the conclusion).

Consistency — A potent weapon in the bluffer's arsenal. Two or more propositions are inconsistent if it's impossible for them to be true at the same time. It's virtually impossible to point out other people's inconsistencies too frequently, but try to avoid having other people point out yours.

Propositions — Simply sentences that are either true or false, like "Pat Sajak is really a hamster," but strangely enough, a question like this, philosophically speaking, isn't a proposition. "Would you like to go to my place and see my collection of French cheeses?" is a proposition. Atomic propositions are propositions that assert something about something else, and, as such, were thought by the Early Wittgenstein (though not, of course, by the Late Wittgenstein) to be fundamentals of language.

Entailment—The relation between the *premises* of a *sound* or *valid* argument and its *conclusion*—if *x* entails *y*, then *y* follows from *x* (it's much more impressive to talk of entailment rather than saying that one thing follows from another).

Conditionals—Propositions showcased into the "if . . . then . . ." format; they're the basic building blocks of logical arguments.

Counterfactuals—A type of *conditional* in which the first part (the "if" clause) is false—such as, "If pigs had wings, then police cruisers would be obsolete." They're interesting to the philosopher because it's difficult to analyze their *truth conditions;* they're handy for the bluffer in that it's a skillful ploy to point out that "I'm not sure how to *interpret* that counterfactual." They're sometimes known as "subjunctive conditionals," generally by people who want you to know they've had some Latin.

Truth Conditions—The conditions under which something is true; altogether too much is made about them, all things considered.

Triviality—Not a general characterization of the whole philosophy subject, but a logical concept. Something is *trivially true* if its truth follows without any special logical inference from something else. Thus, if both *p* and *q* are true, trivially *p* is true. It's surprising how you can unnerve even the most poised individuals by saying, "That's true, but only *trivially* true!"

Rational –
(1) reasoned;
(2) (*math.*) a number that can be expressed as a function of two other numbers;
(3) anything that you yourself might say.

Irrational –
(1) unreasoned;
(2) (*math.*) a number that can't be expressed as a function of two other numbers;
(3) anything that anyone else might say.

Analytic and **Synthetic** – Kant's useful distinction between two types of truth. *Analytic truths* are those which are true solely because meanings of the words they contain independently or the state of the word (such as "All bachelors are unmarried"); *synthetic truths,* on the other hand (such as "Haddocks are never opera singers") are true *or* false according to empirical circumstances (there *might* have been haddocks who performed at La Scala). It's one of the great tragedies of life that analytic truths, although certain and indubitable, are of little use, whereas synthetic truths, although useful, are by no means certain or indubitable. Kant actually disagreed with this, thinking that there could be *a priori* (see below) synthetic truths, such as those found in geometry. But he was wrong, unfortunately.

A priori and **a posteriori** – A similar type of distinction. *A priori* truths can be known independently of any empirical facts; *a posteriori* ones can't.

Necessary and **Contingent**—*Necessary* truths are those which couldn't possibly be otherwise; *contingent* ones aren't. Thus, "Joan Rivers is currently a talk show host" is *contingently* true, whereas "Joan Rivers is Joan Rivers" is *necessarily* true (proof that there can be, unfortunately, necessary truths). Another way of putting this is to say that *necessary* truths are true in all Possible Worlds.

Possible Worlds—The whimsical creation of a certain type of eternally wide-eyed philosopher. A *Possible World* is any state of affairs that could be, but generally isn't.

Idealism—As a philosophical concept, it doesn't mean a concern for the welfare of baby seals (or indeed for the welfare of prominent French actresses concerned with the welfare of baby seals) nor is it a belief in the Brotherhood of Man. Idealism is a concept pioneered by Berkeley, stating that external objects have no real existence distinct from their being perceived. Idealists have lots of difficulty explaining what they really mean by this; they usually say that this doesn't mean that objects are illusory. Idealism is contrasted with

Realism, which is the belief that external objects really are there, after all, and not just when someone's taking some notice of them. Realism, however, is an ambiguous term in philosophy. In the Philosophy of Science, it's the view that scientific laws point to real relations in the physical world; it's contrasted with *Instrumentalism,* the view that scientific laws are merely predictive models. You can also be a Realist about Possible Worlds. That is, you'd insist that Possible Worlds *really* exist, but only *potentially* — which is a lot like saying that, while they *really* exist, they don't *actually* exist. Alvin Plantinga believes this way. In the medieval era, Realism was contrasted with

Nominalism — The position that *Universals* (sometimes also known as *Sortals* — terms like "cat" and "table") don't have an independent existence apart from the collection of their instances — apart, that is, from the actual cats and tables which are parts of the furniture of the world. *Realists,* in this sense, believe that there are Individual Universal Entities which account for our being able to sort the world into coherent groupings of things. Plato was a Realist in this sense (if only in a few others).

Semantics — A useful distinction to be aware of, particularly when talking to computer buffs. You should know the difference between Semantics and Syntax (or Syntactics). You supply a *Semantic* for an argument (or whatever) when you provide a method of translating the symbols it contains into something meaningful; to give a semantic for a language either presupposes or involves a *Theory of Meaning*. By contrast, the *Syntax* is simply the formal grammar of the system — whether the symbols are joined together properly or not. Thus, you can follow the *Syntax* of a system without having the least notion about its *Semantics*. In fact, this is largely what the bluffer is doing in philosophy. He knows, ideally, how to manipulate the terms of the language, as the Late (but not, of course, the Early) Wittgenstein might have put it, but he hasn't got a clue as to what it's really all about, Alfie.

Bluffer's Guides
CENTENNIAL PRESS

The biggest bluff about the *Bluffer's Guides* is the title. These books are full of information — and fun.

NOW IN STOCK — $3.95

Bluff Your Way in Baseball
Bluff Your Way in British Theatre
Bluff Your Way in Computers
Bluff Your Way in the Deep South
Bluff Your Way in Football
Bluff Your Way in Golf
Bluff Your Way in Gourmet Cooking
Bluff Your Way in Hollywood
Bluff Your Way in Japan
Bluff Your Way in Management
Bluff Your Way in Marketing
Bluff Your Way in Music
Bluff Your Way in New York
Bluff Your Way in the Occult
Bluff Your Way in Paris
Bluff Your Way in Public Speaking
Bluff Your Way in Wine
Bluffer's Guide to Bluffing

NEW TITLES

Bluff Your Way in the Great Outdoors
Bluff Your Way in Home Maintenance
Bluff Your Way in Math
Bluff Your Way in Office Politics
Bluff Your Way in Philosophy
Bluff Your Way in Psychology
Bluff Your Way in Sex

To order any of the Bluffer's Guides titles above,
use the order form on the next page.

AVAILABLE SOON

Bluff Your Way in Basketball
Bluff Your Way in Dining Out
Bluff Your Way in Etiquette
Bluff Your Way in Fitness
Bluff Your Way in Las Vegas
Bluff Your Way in London
Bluff Your Way in Marriage
Bluff Your Way in Parenting
Bluff Your Way in Politics
Bluff Your Way in Relationships

Get Bluffer's Guides at your bookstore or use this order form to send for the copies you want. Send it with your check or money order to:

Centennial Press
Box 82087
Lincoln, NE 68501

Title	Quantity	$3.95 Each
Total Enclosed		

Name_____

Address_____

City _____

State_____ Zip_____